CHIMPANZEES

BY DAN GREENBERG

BENCHMARK BOOKS

MARSHALL CAVENDISH
NEW YORK

Series Consultant: James Doherty
General Curator
Bronx Zoo, New York

Benchmark Books
Marshall Cavendish Corporation
99 White Plains Road
Tarrytown, NY 10591–9001

Library of Congress Cataloging-in-Publication data:
Greenberg, Daniel A.
Chimpanzees / Daniel Greenberg.
p. cm.
Includes bibliographical information and index.
Summary: Describes the life of chimpanzees, including social structure, reproduction, and child rearing, use of tools and
ability to solve problems, and loss of habitat.
ISBN 0-7614-1165-8
1. Chimpanzees–Juvenile literature. [1. Chimpanzees.] I. Title.
QL737.P96   G753   2000
599.885–dc21   00-024278

Cover photo: *Animals, Animals*/Anup & Manoj Shah

All photographs are used by permission and through the courtesy of *Animals, Animals*
Anup Shah: 4; C. Bromhall: 8, 15, 22, 27; A. & M. Shah: 9, 10 (bottom), 14 (right), 33; Mike Birkhead: 10 (top), 17;
Bruce Davidson: 13, 34, 40, 41, 42; M. Colbeck: 14 (left); Zig Leszczynski: 18; Stewart D. Halperin: 20; Dani/Jeske: 24;
H. S. Terrace: 25; Ken Cole: 29; Michael Leach: 30; S. Turner: 35; Jerry Cooke: 37; Raymond A. Mendez: 38;
Corbis Images: 16.

Printed in the United States

1 3 5 6 4 2

CONTENTS

1 INTRODUCING CHIMPANZEES
.... 5

2 LIFE IN A COMMUNITY
.... 12

3 FOOD AND LANGUAGE
.... 23

4 A CHIMPANZEE'S LIFE
.... 28

5 FRIENDS IN TROUBLE
.... 36

GLOSSARY
.... 44

FIND OUT MORE
.... 46

INDEX
.... 48

1

INTRODUCING CHIMPANZEES

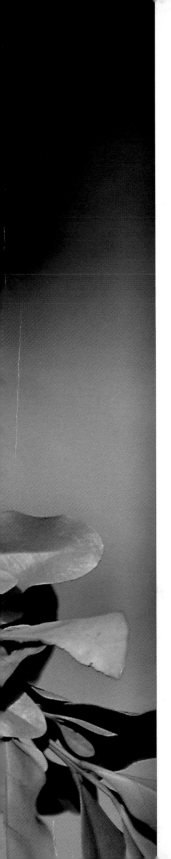

Lucy was thirsty. She went to the refrigerator and poured herself a cold drink. Then she settled down in her favorite chair. There was nothing good on TV, so Lucy opened a magazine. Ah, here was something interesting: a photo of a poodle. "That dog," Lucy said, in sign language.

Would it surprise you that Lucy is eight years old? Probably not. But to learn that Lucy is a chimpanzee—now that *is* surprising! How is it that a chimp can do all of these amazing things?

THIS CHIMP IN THE SWEETWATERS SANCTUARY IN KENYA SNACKS ON FRESH GREEN LEAVES.

Chimps are more like human beings than any other animal. Chimps smile, laugh, frown, and cry. They greet each other. They notice themselves in the mirror. They tease, boast, act silly, and even tickle one another.

How similar are chimpanzees and humans?
DNA is the master chemical that contains the "operating instructions" for every cell in the body. It tells the cells which chemicals to make. These chemicals decide such things as how you look, whether you are male or female, how tall you are, and even perhaps, how you behave. The DNA of chimps is more similar to the DNA of humans than that of any other animal. In fact, chimp and human DNA has been shown to be over 98 percent alike.

CHIMPS ARE SMALLER THAN GORILLAS, THE LARGEST OF THE GREAT APES. WHILE SMALLER THAN A FULL-GROWN HUMAN, CHIMPS ARE TWO TO THREE TIMES STRONGER.

THIS SKELETON SHOWS THE
LENGTH OF A CHIMP'S ARMS,
LEGS, HANDS, AND FEET—
PERFECT FOR CLIMBING AND
SWINGING FROM TREES.
CHIMPS CANNOT STAND
UPRIGHT FOR VERY LONG
BECAUSE THEIR SPINE AND LEGS
ARE CURVED. STANDING
UPRIGHT PUTS TOO MUCH
STRAIN ON THE SPINE.

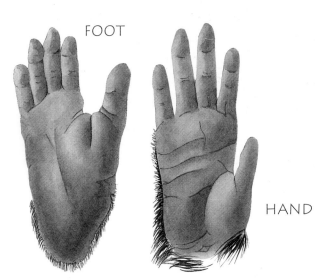

FOOT

HAND

WHEN THE CHIMPANZEE IS
CLIMBING, THE FOOT'S BIG TOE
ACTS LIKE A THUMB TO HELP
THE ANIMAL GRASP BRANCHES.

7

Both chimps and humans are *primates*. Both have large brains, use tools, and have language. Humans and chimps can even get the same diseases, such as polio and AIDS. They also share a very complex social life.

On the other hand, there are many differences between humans and chimps. Chimps, and their close cousins the *bonobos*, are shorter than humans and a lot stronger. Chimps' brains are not as large as humans, so their intelligence is more limited. They communicate in simple ways. The tools they make and use are extremely crude.

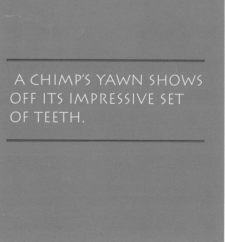

A CHIMP'S YAWN SHOWS OFF ITS IMPRESSIVE SET OF TEETH.

THIS ADULT
CHIMP SEEMS TO
BE IN A
THOUGHTFUL
MOOD.
SCIENTISTS
CANNOT AGREE
ON JUST HOW
INTELLIGENT
CHIMPS ARE.

CHIMPANZEES SPEND MUCH OF THEIR TIME IN TREES. THEY SLEEP IN THEM AT NIGHT. DURING THE DAY, THEY MAY SEARCH FOR FOOD IN THEIR BRANCHES OR, AS SHOWN HERE, SIMPLY SWING FROM THEM FOR FUN.

10

Finally, chimps are much less successful in *colonizing* the world than humans. There are billions of humans all over the planet. Chimps now live in only a few small regions in central Africa. There are less than 100,000 chimps in the world today.

2
LIFE IN A COMMUNITY

It is sunrise in the African rain forest. High in the trees, the chimpanzee *community* sleeps. Chimps live mostly in thick forests like this one. But chimps can survive equally well in other *habitats*. Some chimps live in mountain forests as high as 10,000 feet (3,000 meters). Other chimps make their home in the wide-open African savanna.

THIS CHIMP NEST IS A COMPLICATED TANGLE OF BRANCHES, TWIGS, AND LEAVES. CHIMPS MAKE A FRESH NEST EVERY NIGHT.

12

HABITAT

CHIMPANZEES
AND PYGMY
CHIMPANZEES
LIVE IN CENTRAL
AFRICA.

KEY

COMMON CHIMPANZEE

PYGMY CHIMPANZEE

CHIMPS CAN ADAPT TO DIFFERENT HABITATS, SUCH AS THE TROPICAL FOREST OF ZAIRE (LEFT) OR THE DRIER SAVANNA OF KENYA (RIGHT).

A chimp community may have from fifteen to one hundred members. At any time, groups, called parties, may split off from the community or join together again. Young *bachelor* males may travel alone. Groups of females and juveniles often roam the forest in the company of a single male. But at nightfall, the groups often meet again to sleep in the trees.

14

A BACHELOR MALE STRETCHES HIS LONG ARM TO GRAB A PIECE OF FRUIT.

JANE GOODALL

IN 1960 YOUNG JANE GOODALL WENT TO TANZANIA TO STUDY CHIMPS. SHE HAD NO SCIENTIFIC TRAINING. BUT SHE WAS SMART, TOUGH, AND HONEST. OVER THE NEXT FORTY YEARS, GOODALL STUDIED CHIMPANZEES. SHE BECAME A FAMOUS SCIENTIST, HONORED ALL OVER THE WORLD. GOODALL WAS THE FIRST PERSON TO DISCOVER THAT

* CHIMPANZEES MAKE AND USE TOOLS
* CHIMPANZEES HUNT AND EAT MEAT
* CHIMPANZEES CAN SEE THEMSELVES IN A MIRROR AND HAVE AN IDEA OF THEIR OWN SELF
* CHIMPANZEES CAN PASS ON IDEAS TO OTHERS
* CHIMPANZEES HAVE A RICH AND COMPLEX SOCIAL LIFE.

Each group is organized according to rank. A single *dominant male* is the leader. All others must show him respect. Friends must show loyalty or risk attack.

The leader gains his rank through a dramatic show of *display* behavior. During a display, a male will do all sorts of things—stomp, kick, howl, throw sticks, make faces—to scare his fellow chimps.

WHEN FIGHTING FOR POWER, CHIMPS STAMP OR SLAP THE GROUND BEFORE ATTACKING.

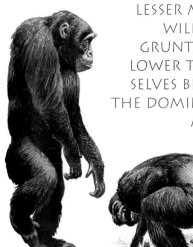

LESSER MALES WILL BOB, GRUNT, AND LOWER THEM- SELVES BEFORE THE DOMINANT MALE.

A MALE CHIMP MAY USE A WEAPON TO THREATEN ANOTHER MALE.

CHIMPS OFTEN SET OUT IN SMALL GROUPS DURING THE DAY TO SEARCH FOR FOOD.

17

Once in command, the leader controls the group's mating and feeding behavior. He does most of the mating and decides where the group will forage for food and when to groom and play.

Playing is important to a chimp community. Youngsters under the age of ten like to play. Like humans, chimps often

CHIMPS LOVE TO PLAY. HERE, A BABY IS ENTERTAINED BY ITS OLDER RELATIVE.

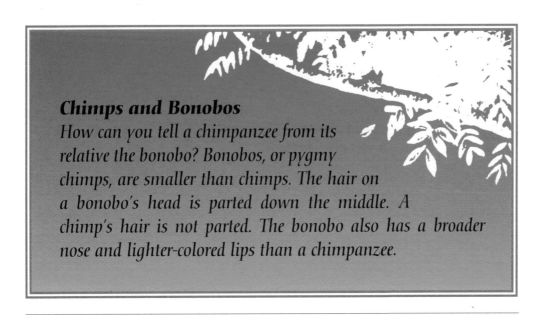

Chimps and Bonobos

How can you tell a chimpanzee from its relative the bonobo? Bonobos, or pygmy chimps, are smaller than chimps. The hair on a bonobo's head is parted down the middle. A chimp's hair is not parted. The bonobo also has a broader nose and lighter-colored lips than a chimpanzee.

play with chimps their own age. They fight, wrestle, chase, tickle, and hide from one another. Sometimes, adults will join in their games.

Grooming is important for chimps of all ages, too. All chimps spend a large part of each day grooming. Mothers groom children. Adults of high and low rank take turns grooming each other. Grooming not only keeps chimps' coats clean and free of parasites, it works to calm and soothe. After a squabble or disagreement, the injured parties often sit down to groom. Soon, all seems to have been forgotten.

A GROUP OF CHIMPS GROOM ONE ANOTHER. GROOMING INVOLVES REMOVING BUGS, PARASITES, AND DIRT FROM THE FUR.

21

3
FOOD AND LANGUAGE

At midday the forest is quiet. Small parties of chimps rustle the leaves, searching for food. In other habitats, chimps may eat plant foods such as seeds, roots, leaves, and flowers. But here in the rain forest the main foods are bananas, berries, and other fruits. Chimpanzees also eat eggs, insects, and sometimes meat.

Suddenly a cry goes up. Loud *pant-hoots* echo through the trees. The chimps are excited: a nearby group has made a kill. Chimps come running from every direction to join the feast. As hunters, male chimps sometimes stalk their prey, which can include bushpigs, monkeys, and bats. In other cases, chimps steal a kill from nearby baboons. Once a kill is made, there is much scrambling and begging to get the meat. Some will get a share; others will go without.

AN ADULT MALE GATHERS FOOD IN LIBERIA.

Chimps eat insects, too. To catch termites, chimps make tools. First they strip the leaves from a twig. Then they shove the twig tool down a termite hole. When pulled up, the tool is covered with termites. Chimps also use tools to get ants, honey, and other foods. Chimps even make sponge tools out of crumpled leaves to get water.

Using tools isn't the only way chimps show their intelligence. Chimps have a highly developed communication system. The pant-hoot is only

THIS CHIMP HAS USED A STICK TO PULL INSECTS FROM THEIR UNDERGROUND NEST.

one of more than thirty different calls that chimps use to communicate feelings such as fear (Wraa!), enjoyment (lip smack), and distress (Hoo!).

. . .

WASHOE'S LANGUAGE

MANY SCIENTISTS HAVE ATTEMPTED TO TEACH CHIMPS HUMAN LANGUAGE. THE MOST SUCCESSFUL EFFORTS BEGAN WITH A CHIMP NAMED WASHOE IN NEVADA. BECAUSE THE ACT OF FORMING WORDS IS DIFFICULT FOR A CHIMP, WASHOE WAS TAUGHT AMERICAN SIGN LANGUAGE (ASL) USING HAND GESTURES. BEFORE LONG, WASHOE HAD LEARNED 132 DIFFERENT ASL WORDS. WASHOE CREATED SENTENCES, ANSWERED QUESTIONS, AND EVEN INVENTED A FEW NEW ASL WORDS OF HER OWN. WASHOE ALSO TAUGHT A TOTAL OF FIFTY-EIGHT ASL WORDS TO A YOUNG CHIMP NAMED LOULIS WHOM SHE HAD ADOPTED.

. . .

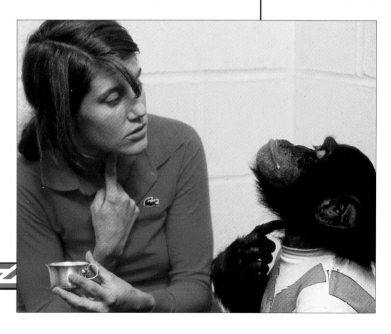

Chimps use their faces and bodies to express them-selves, too. When fighting, a chimp may smash sticks against a tree to show frustration. Community members will greet long-lost friends with hugs and kisses to show how much they were missed. The loser in a squabble will show it is sorry by approaching in a low, skulking

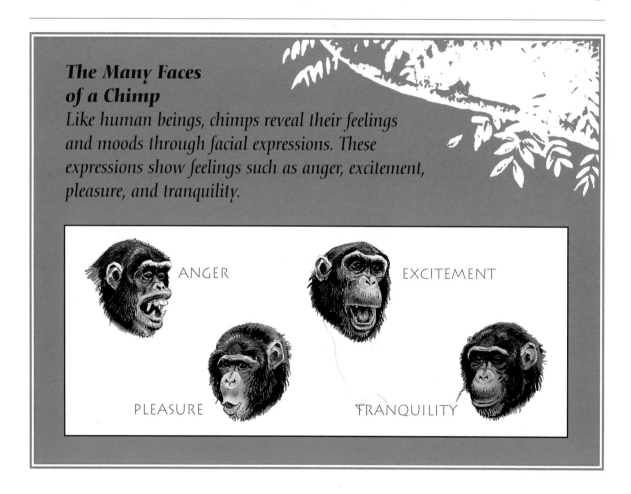

The Many Faces of a Chimp
Like human beings, chimps reveal their feelings and moods through facial expressions. These expressions show feelings such as anger, excitement, pleasure, and tranquility.

ANGER

EXCITEMENT

PLEASURE

TRANQUILITY

A FEMALE CHIMP SCREAMS AND RUSHES TOWARD A MALE WHO IS THREATENING HER BABY. HER SCREAM IS MEANT TO SCARE THE MALE AWAY AND TO ALERT HER RELATIVES.

posture. When the winner touches the loser's extended hand, all seems to be forgiven.

Further proof of chimps' intelligence is their ability to plan and deceive. Take the case of Figan, a male named and observed by scientist Jane Goodall. As a young chimp, Figan watched another chimp named Mike intimidate others by banging garbage can lids together. So what did Figan do? He practiced garbage can banging—on his own, in secret. Years later, Figan would use this and other intimidating tactics to take over as leader of the community.

4
A CHIMP'S LIFE

Until now, five-year-old Fifi has had an ideal childhood. Fifi was first observed and named by scientist Jane Goodall when she was born. Until now, Fifi has stayed close to Flo, her gentle and caring mother. As a young chimp, Fifi loved to play tickle games with her mother. But Fifi's world is beginning to change.

When Flo gives birth to a new baby, Fifi will suddenly be on her own for the first time. No longer will her mother come running

A BABY CHIMPANZEE IMITATES ITS MOTHER.

CHIMPS STAY
WITH THEIR
MOTHERS
LONGER THAN
MOST ANIMALS--
ANOTHER THING
THEY HAVE IN
COMMON WITH
HUMAN BEINGS.

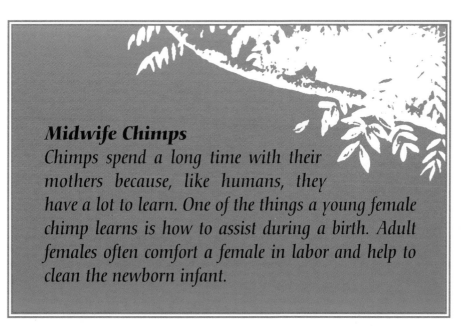

Midwife Chimps

Chimps spend a long time with their mothers because, like humans, they have a lot to learn. One of the things a young female chimp learns is how to assist during a birth. Adult females often comfort a female in labor and help to clean the newborn infant.

every time Fifi whimpers. Fifi will grow to enjoy the baby. She will cuddle and play with it whenever she can.

Fifi will remain close to her mother and family for many years. But at age ten, Fifi's life will change again. The pink swelling around her rump will signal that Fifi is maturing. Over the next two years Fifi will begin to mate with males. These early matings will be unsuccessful. But by

. . .

LOVE THAT BABY

CHIMPANZEE MOTHERS
AREN'T THE ONLY ONES
WHO ENJOY BABIES. THE
ARRIVAL OF A NEW BABY
SEEMS TO DELIGHT MOST
OF THE CHIMPS IN A
COMMUNITY. ADULTS
WILL GO OUT OF THEIR
WAY TO PLAY WITH AN
INFANT. BABY CHIMPS
SEEM ESPECIALLY TO ENJOY
BEING TICKLED.

. . .

age thirteen, Fifi will be old enough to become pregnant.

Young male chimps must listen, learn, and wait. As they mature, they will struggle for power. Their display behaviors toward other males decide how high their rank in the community will be. The loudest and fiercest male may someday become the dominant male.

Once Fifi has her first baby, a pattern will begin. From then on she will give birth every five years or so. By age thirty-three she will begin to slow down and will then live out her days helping others in the community until an old age of about forty.

Male chimps live to about the same age. When a male chimp is old enough, he will challenge the leader. This is a high-stakes game. If the youth wins, he takes control of the community. If he loses, he may lose his

A YOUNG
CHIMP
HAS FUN
SWINGING
FROM
BRANCHES.

EACH CHIMP GROUP HAS A DOMINANT MALE AS ITS LEADER. THIS
DOMINANT MALE KEEPS WATCH OVER HIS TERRITORY.

rank. He will then be driven out of the community and forced to live on his own.

As the new leader, the young male has his pick of females for mating. Lower-ranking males, on the other hand, need to be sly to mate successfully. They may take females who are too young or too old. Or they may sneak away with a desired female when the leader isn't looking.

MALE AND FEMALE CHIMPS FORM BONDS THAT LAST AS LONG AS THE FEMALE'S MATING PERIOD—A FEW DAYS. HERE, A MALE AND FEMALE PAIR GROOM EACH OTHER.

5

FRIENDS IN TROUBLE

Like many other primates, chimpanzees are an endangered species. Each day, the number of chimps in the wild decreases. Most scientists blame the problem on a rival primate—human beings.

People harm chimps in many ways. Hunters kill chimps for meat. *Poachers* capture chimps to be used as pets or in shows. Other chimps are used in medical research projects. Meanwhile, chimp habitats are being lost at a rapid pace.

A CHIMP PERFORMS IN A SHOW. WHILE THIS MAY SEEM CUTE TO THE AUDIENCE, IT IS ACTUALLY CRUEL TO THE ANIMAL.

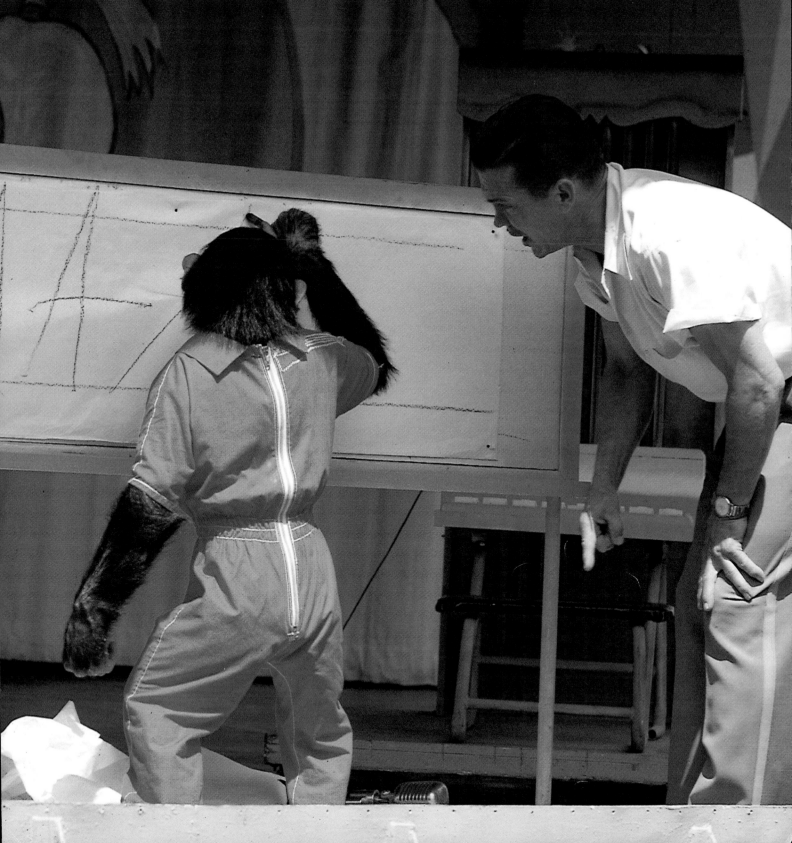

CHIMPS ARE STILL KEPT FOR USE IN MEDICAL EXPERIMENTS.

Forests are cut down. Roads and towns are built. Pollution makes habitats unlivable for chimps.

Can anything be done? The future for chimps may not be as dark as it once seemed. International laws have been passed to protect chimps. National parks have been created as preserves for chimps. Medical research programs have stopped using wild chimps in their projects. But hunting, poaching, and habitat loss remain serious problems for chimp populations.

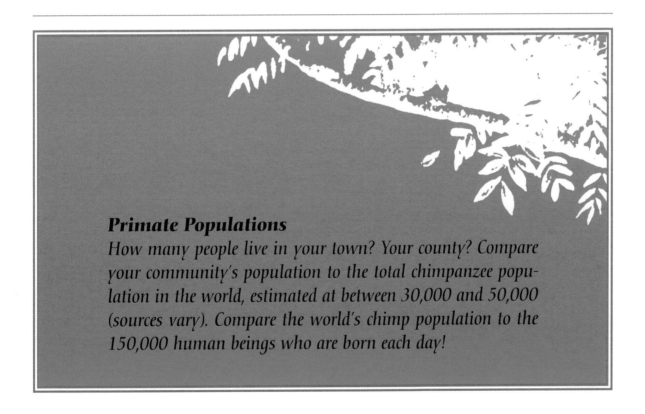

Primate Populations

How many people live in your town? Your county? Compare your community's population to the total chimpanzee population in the world, estimated at between 30,000 and 50,000 (sources vary). Compare the world's chimp population to the 150,000 human beings who are born each day!

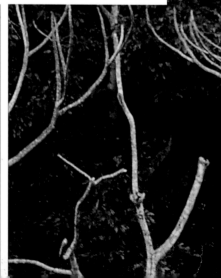

THIS IS THE ITURI RAIN FOREST IN ZAIRE—HOME
TO CHIMPANZEES AND MANY OTHER ANIMALS—
BEFORE DEFORESTATION (RIGHT) AND AFTER (LEFT).

Habitat loss is a particularly tough problem for scientists. Even if we could eliminate all hunting and poaching right now, chimps would still be threatened by land development. To survive and grow, chimp communities need more undeveloped wilderness, not less.

What can be done to help chimps? Organizations such as the Jane Goodall Institute raise money to help chimps in different ways. They work to change laws and minds. Slowly, people are beginning to realize that chimpanzees really are worth saving.

A YOUNG CHIMP STOPS FOR A SNACK IN THE ITURI RAIN FOREST. WORK MUST BE DONE TO SAVE THIS RAIN FOREST, AND OTHERS LIKE IT, OR CHIMPS WILL HAVE EVEN FEWER PLACES TO LIVE.

AIDS: Acquired Immune Deficiency Syndrome—a disorder transmitted through the blood in which the immune system is not able to defend against common infections.

ASL: American Sign Language—a language used primarily by people with hearing impairments, which relies on signs rather than words.

bachelor: A single male chimpanzee.

bonobo: A pygmy chimpanzee; a small variety of chimp that lives along the Zaire River.

colonize: To settle in, or inhabit, a place.

community: A group of twenty to one hundred chimpanzees that live together.

display: Behavior of male chimpanzees that is designed to intimidate; includes stomping, pounding, shouting, and throwing objects.

DNA: Deoxyribonucleic acid—the genetic material inside every cell of an organism that holds the information for carrying out life processes and passing on traits.

dominant male: The leader of a chimpanzee group who controls the group's feeding and mating behavior.

grooming: A calming, soothing behavior in which chimps stroke and clean each other's fur.

habitat: The place where a plant or animal normally lives and grows.

higher primates: Monkeys, apes, and human beings.

lower primates: Bush babies, lemurs, tarsiers, and others.

pant–hoot: One of more than thirty chimp calls uttered to indicate excitement.

poacher: A person who hunts chimpanzees (or other animals) illegally.

primate: The order of mammals that includes monkeys, prosimians (such as lemurs and bush babies), apes, and humans.

BOOKS

Banks, Martin. *Chimpanzee*. Austin, TX: Raintree/Steck–Vaughn, 2000.

Berger, Gotthart. *Monkeys and Apes*. New York: Arco Publishing, 1985.

Elwood, Ann. *Chimpanzees & Bonobos*. Mankato, MN: Creative Education, 1991.

Goodall, Jane. *The Chimpanzee Family Book*. Saxonville, MA: Picture Book Studio, 1989.

Goodall, Jane. *The Chimpanzees of Gombe*. Cambridge, MA: Harvard University Press, 1986.

Sterry, Paul. *Monkeys & Apes*, New York: Smithmark Books, 1994.

WEBSITES

Animal Diversity Web
http://animaldiversity.ummz.umich.edu/index.html

The Jane Goodall Institute
http://www.janegoodall.org

Chimpanzees, by Eric Johansen
http://www.tc.umn.edu/~joha0103/chimp.html

Chimps.org: The Chimp Database (links to zoos around the United States)
http://chimps.org

Chimps, Inc. (learn about real chimps online)
http://www.chimps-inc.com

Chimp World
http://millennium.simplenet.com/chimpworld/

World Wildlife Fund
http://www.wwf.org

Dan Greenberg has written numerous books for readers of all ages, on topics that range from science to math to baseball. His best-known series of humor books has ten titles, including *Comic Strip Math* and *Comic Strip Grammar*. He lives in New York with his wife and children.

INDEX

Page numbers for photos are in **boldface**.

baboon, 24

bonobo (pygmy chimpanzee), 8, 13, 19

chimpanzee, **4**, **8**, **9**, **10**, **17**, **37**, **43**

  body, **7**, 11, 19

  brain, 8

  communication, 8, 23, 25

  community, 12, 14

  disease, 8

  display behavior, 16, **17**

  dominant male, 16, **17**, 18, 32, **34**, 35

  expressiveness, 6, **9**, 26–27

  female, 14, **27**, 28, **30**, 31, 32

  food, 16, **22**, 23–24

  foot, **7**, 11

  grooming, 16, 19, **20**, **35**,

  habitat, 12, **13**, **14**, 36, 38, 39, **40–41**, **42**

  hand, **7**

  hunting, 16, 23–24

  intelligence, 8, 16, 25, 27

  language, 5, 8, 25

  life span, 32

  male, 14, **15**, 16, **27**, 32, **34**, 35

  mating, 16, 31–32, 35

  nest, **13**

  playing, 16, 18–19, **18**, 32

  population, 11, 39

  size, **6**

  skeleton, **7**

  sleep, 12, 14,

  social behavior, 8, 16, 26, 27, 32

  strength, 6

  thumb, 7, 11

  tool use, 8, 16, 24, **24**

  war, 18

  young, 28, **29**, **30**, 31, 32, **33**

DNA, 6

Goodall, Jane, 16, **16**, 18, 27, 28

gorilla, **6**

humans, 6, **6**, 8, 11, 36, 39

Jane Goodall Institute, 43

medical research, 36, **38**, 39

poaching, 36, 39

primates, 8, 36